STAN L

A Life Well Lived

TIM D. WASHINGTON

Table of Contents

AN OVERVIEW OF STAN LEE'S LIFE

Stanley Martin Lieber (Stan Lee) is one of the most influential people in the history of comics in America and the world at large. The famous comic book writer, producer, editor, and publisher was born on December 28, 1922, in New York. His parents were immigrant Jews from Romania. Stan Lee helped us see things from a different perspective, thanks to his amazing works in the creation of the greatest superhero characters.

Throughout his career, Stan Lee worked with other talented minds such as Jack Kirby and Steve Ditko to create captivating superhero characters such as Hulk, Fantastic 4, Thor, Iron Man, Spiderman, Daredevil, The Avengers, Doctor Strange, and X-Men. If you are a fan of superhero characters from Marvel Comics, you are definitely a fan of Stan Lee's works. Marvel Comics started out as a small-sized publishing house before becoming the multi-billion business that it is today. The company has always introduced its works by giving credit to Stan Lee. This habit turned out to be the company's method of doing business.

Fans of movies and comic books have many people to thank, especially the incredible writers like Bob Kane, Jack Kirby, and Steve Ditko. We've already mentioned the last two, so let's talk about Bob Kane. If you love the legendary Batman character, then you have enjoyed one of the fascinating works of Bob Kane. Just like these writers, Stan Lee managed to become one of the best comic writers. In fact, he became famous for writing most Marvel-published characters and series in the 1960s.

One of Stan's greatest aspirations as a youngster was to become a novelist, but things didn't work out his way due to unforeseen circumstances. However, he managed to save a genre that was on the verge of disappearing and made it one of the most-loved Western genres in the entertainment industry, just like humor and horror.

Like many people who ended up getting positions in organizations, Stan Lee first worked at the Timely Comics publisher as an intern. This was towards the end of the 1940s before the publisher was renamed from Timely Comics to Marvel Comics. Stan's first project was a 2-page cartoon of Jack Kirby and Joe Simon's Captain America. However, the Marvel Universe didn't become famous until 1961.

Everything changed for good when Stan partnered with Kirby to create amazing stories of heroes with superpowers, The Fantastic Four. The story featured Sue Storm, Johnny Storm, Ben Grimm, and Reed Richards. These scientists traveled through space using a rocket and ended up acquiring special powers because of exposure to cosmic rays. They used their powers to advocate for justice. With their new powers, the scientists embarked on many adventures that involved working with other characters with superpowers to defeat villains.

When the publisher realized that the Fantastic Four was successful, Stan Lee became the key source of inspiration and the creator of more superheroes. Since then, Stan collaborated with great writers like Kirby, Don Heck, and Ditko to write and create more superhero characters. Today, many people remember Stan Lee and his colleagues for the creation of amazing comic characters such as Hulk, Spiderman, Iron Man, X-Men, and Doctor Strange.

Human-Like Comic Characters Based on Great Ideas

Martin Goodman's decision to transform Timely Comics to Marvel Comics in 1961 wasn't the only good thing that happened that year. The publisher also published the initial issue of the Fantastic Four in 1961. Jack Kirby was responsible for drawings, and Stan Lee was the chief editor. Although Stan Lee had already formed some characters while working for Timely Comics, he started gaining popularity after the launch of the Fantastic Four.

Stan realized that his work was attracting the attention of many comic fans, so he decided to create more comic characters to meet the needs of the public. His work got easier because many people were already appreciating what he was doing. There was no doubt that his audience wanted more, so he decided to give them what they wanted.

Of course, Stan paid a lot of attention to the powers possessed by his characters, but he also focused on other important things that contributed to his success. If you ask people who are experts in semiotics and literature, they will tell you that successful storytellers mainly use basic dramas. That's exactly what made Stan succeed in the early days of his career. He used simple and innovative tricks to capture the reader's attention.

His characters' superpowers definitely played a crucial role, but he was keen to bring out the human aspects hidden behind the suits, capes, and masks worn by the superheroes he created. Just like real human beings, Stan's superheroes had some shortcomings as well. He didn't give his audience characters who were always beautiful, victorious, or flawless female athletes.

In simple terms, Stan's superheroes were similar to real humans who faced the same problems as ordinary people do.

Another fascinating thing about the characters created by Stan Lee for Marvel Comics is that they had exaggerated gestures. Stan insisted on these gestures because of his passion for the theatre. He believed that the gestures played a vital role in helping people understand what the characters were expressing without relying on his declamation.

Many people were eager to know how Stan managed to be so productive and successful. Well, the truth behind all this was how well he wrote. He would start his story with a simple plot with descriptions of what would transpire on each page. The next step was to hand the plot to the person responsible for the drawings. After receiving the drawings, Stan would then add the texts and dialogues.

Based on his agreement with the artist, the drawings needed to support each scene's performance and fun to read. The main goal was to make sure that readers could understand what each character expressed with almost no help from the declamation. Stan wanted everything to be as entertaining as it sounded.

Over 60 Superheroes and Unforgettable Villains

In case you didn't know, Stan Lee is responsible for creating most Marvel Cinematic Universe characters and many of them were created in the 1960s. There are only a few exceptions, including the Guardian of the Galaxy characters, and Captain America. Even the fictional superhero Groot was conceptualized by Stan Lee.

The original X-men series needed more hands to achieve commercial success and popularity among the fans of comic superheroes. Stan needed help to create characters like Professor Xavier, Iceman, Beast, Jean Grey, Angel, and Cyclops. Other characters like Storm and Logan came later. Stan is also known for introducing the first fictional superhero of color. He created Black Panther and the Falcon. Additionally, some of the best American television series based on fictional characters were also created by Stan Lee. These include Nick Fury, Agent Carter, Daredevil, Inhuman, and SHIELD.

Where there are great heroes, you can expect to come across great villains as well. One of the reasons why Stan's stories are so intriguing is that they come with tough evil villains. These villains make his stories more interesting to read because they bring interesting twists and challenges. For instance, a story featuring a monarch who wears an iron mask and fights an evil character to save his mother is more interesting than a story of a crybaby pilot made of rocks.

Stan Lee was aware of the incredible role played by villains in comic stories, so he decided to create amazing villain characters such as Magneto and Doctor Doom. Other evil characters created by Stan include the Scarlet Witch, Black

Widow, and Hawkeye. Generally, Lee learned the art of using family problems to create several villains with a fascinating origin story. After writing for many years, he gained a lot of experience and was able to infuse romance, melodrama, adventures, and other aspects of culture into his characters and stories. For this reason, many of his characters have been successful in switching sides.

Lee was a smart creator with unparalleled creativity, which enabled him to create ridiculously complacent superheroes like Spider-Man and many others. If you've seen Spider-Man, you'll agree that he is simply a bully wearing a suit. Stan also used his creative skills to create various thematic characters, namely Birdman, Ape-Man, Ani-Men, and Cat-Man.

There are many stories featuring characters created by Stan Lee. One of the best stories based on the works of Stan Lee is a thrilling circus featuring the Hulk. In that story clowns and acrobats want to capture Hulk.

Other Aspirations

Stan Lee will always be remembered for playing a very important role in creating some of the best comic cartoon characters we know today. He didn't rest until he achieved his dreams, which included becoming an actor. If you have watched any film based on his characters, you can attest to the fact that he managed to achieve his dreams.

His acting journey began when he appeared in the 1989 American superhero film, *The Trial of the Incredible Hulk*. In the film, Stan represented a juror during Banner's trial. Since then, Stan appeared in films featuring Marvel characters. One of his greatest milestones was his reality show titled "Who Wants to Be a Superhero."

Another incredible achievement by Stan was the inception of the Stan Lee Foundation in 2010. The foundation's key areas of focus include literature, arts, and education. It helped him achieve a number of goals, including access to devices and literary programs for all people regardless of their background, color, and age. Stan's foundation is also famous for promoting diversity, culture, creativity, education, literature, integrity, and arts, to reach all people, especially learners and creators. Only determined people like Stan can achieve such milestones.

Chapter 1:

PARENTS AND FAMILY

Stan Lee's father and mother came to America in the early years of the 20th century as immigrants. His Romanian father was born in 1886 and arrived at NYC harbor in 1905. Lee's father was initially known by the name Hyman which later changed to Jacob or Jack. He was only 19 years old when he arrived at the harbor and was accompanied by a relative called Abraham on his way to New York. At that time, there were millions of Jewish Immigrants that entered the U.S. after several years of pogroms against Jews in Russia and European countries. Many Jews lost their lives and were deprived of their rights. In 1880, the number of immigrants in the U.S was estimated to be 5,000, but this number increased to 258,000 in 1907. America received more than 2.7 million European immigrants from 1875 to 1924.

It was extremely hard to have a decent life when Hyman left Romania, a country located between Austria and Hungary (north), Serbia (west), Bulgaria (south), and Russia (east). The young Hyman Lieber left the country when Carol I was the reigning monarch. Carol, I ruled the nation of Romania from 1881 to 1914. It is said that Hyman and his friend Abraham each spent approximately 179 rubles, which makes 90 dollars. This was a huge sum of money to pay for a trip from Europe to the U.S. The good news is that it was not in vain because the benefits turned out to be more than the value of money they spent during their voyage.

Out of the 179 rubles, the two travelers showed 50 rubles ($25) to the immigration staff at Ellis Island to prove that they could start a new life and survive if they were allowed to stay in America. Hyman and his friend arrived in the U.S in one of the first and largest groups of Romanians who were looking for a better life in America. It's estimated that about 145,000 Romanians left for America between the 1890s and 1920s.

The main reason way most Romanians were determined to reach America despite the long voyage was to enjoy economic stability, wealth, and religious freedom. In fact, the first Eastern Europeans and the groups that followed them moved to America, hoping to get decent wages and even save some money. Their ultimate goal was to save their earnings and eventually go back home and purchase land. Overall, the number of people who moved from Romania to America was fewer than the immigrants from other countries.

Jewish immigrants from Romania and other European countries had a more dramatic experience compared to other people who were immigrating to America at that time. Romanian Jews chose to move to America for good because of discrimination. Life was very tough for Jewish men because discrimination contributed to fewer jobs that could help them earn enough money to enjoy a decent life.

The monarchy made life extremely difficult because Jews were not allowed to become lawyers or study medicine. In addition, the monarchy banned rabbinical seminaries. The worst part is that Romanian Jews were considered to be foreigners or aliens, even if their families had been around for many years. Many of the people who decided to travel from Romania to the U.S testified that it was extremely difficult to live in their home country as minorities. They were always subjected to discrimination because of their ethnic background and religious practices. It was a harsh world to live in, so the only option they had was to move out.

It was normal for those in power to abuse their powers. For instance, a law was passed in 1890, making the Jews second class citizens. As a result, Romanian Jews were prohibited from accessing education. This law had devastating effects on the Jews, including psychological problems such as trauma.

The law wasn't the only problem faced by Jews at that time. Romanian Jews were also subjected to violence almost every day. There were pogroms that led to many anti-Jewish uprisings and robbery with violence. Unfortunately, the people who were supposed to enforce the law like the army and the police were reluctant to stop the riots and other violent behaviors against the Jews.

According to the accounts of historians, Romania was facing many problems in the final years of the 19th century leading to more problems. A good example is the terrible economic depression, which was followed by a lot of violence. This included anti-Semitic uprisings in Bârlad, Buzău, Botoşani, Bucharest, and Iaşi. There was a small number of Romanians in the U.S, so the news of the violence didn't reach America to prompt media scrutiny.

About 6,000 migrants decided to return home in the early years of the twentieth century, but Hyman was determined to start a life in New York. Some immigrants from Eastern Europe even traveled to their home countries and returned to America several times with ease. Of course, they were taking tremendous risks, but everything they did was worthwhile. The amount of money they got from the manufacturing industry was enough to transform their lives as well as their families. After the end of the initial burst, a few people from Romania moved to the U.S for the next 25 years. There was no significant increase in the numbers until the country was threatened by the Nazis during the Second World War.

Life wasn't easy for the first group of Romanian immigrants who managed to reach the U.S. They faced hardships that put their traditional practices and family values to the test. Another major challenge for the immigrants was the lack of skills. Most of them worked as laborers without the required skills, so they had difficulty working in American cities where there were manufacturing plants and mills. It was a dangerous job, as evident by the frequent industrial accidents among immigrant laborers. The risks of working without the appropriate skills included injuries and even casualties.

However, life in NYC was better for Romanian Jews compared to what they had experienced in their home country. They saw a great opportunity and took advantage of it to achieve the American Dream. Of course, they faced the same challenges that were faced by other immigrants like housing problems and poverty, but the benefits were more than the challenges. Once they entered America, Romanian Jews started to enjoy the long-awaited religious freedom. Moreover, they were safe from the cruel violence against Jews in Romania. America was generally welcoming.

Like other single young men, Hyman had decided to leave his home country and family just to earn. In most cases, the young unmarried workers would live in groups in various boarding homes. Others chose to live with other immigrant families from Romania. Hyman and other young men would meet at different locations such as churches, saloons, and local restaurants.

During their stay in America, Jewish immigrants also faced the risk of being discriminated against, so they formed groups with their countrymen. This provided them with some form of protection from anti-Semitism. Another significant problem faced by Jewish immigrants was the language barrier. The groups they formed allowed them to stay together and face English speakers who were potential threats.

The Romanian-born British and American novelist Maurice Samuel once explained the kind of experience he had after visiting a restaurant that was mainly frequented by Romanian Jews. According to him, people who visited the restaurant would eat, drink, and play. They ate kashkaval, beigalech, karnatzlech, and mămăliga. That restaurant was a great place to have fun while talking in their Romanian language. People would tell incredible stories about Jewish heritage.

However, it was easy to notice the worries and regrets the Romanians were dealing with because of the crushing anti-Jewish pogroms. Some storytellers would actually shed tears while telling their nostalgic stories, which showed the devastating effects of anti-Semitism.

Upon reaching New York City, Hyman and Abraham found a place in the cloth manufacturing industry. They were lucky because the garment sector was looking for workers. At that time, about 65% of the Jewish immigrants had already acquired useful skills of craftsmen. However, it's hard to tell whether

Hyman worked in the clothing sector or got additional training in his home country. This was extremely difficult in Romania because of the harsh laws, anti-Jewish educational system, and biased business practices that worked against Jews in Romania. According to one historian, there was a high demand for tailors in Manhattan, so the immigrants would acquire that skill immediately after arriving in the U.S.

1st Generation Family

Many 1st generation families during the era of the Liebers were reluctant to share a lot of information about their past and their voyage to the United States. Of course, many people who immigrated to America at that time came with different cultural practices from their home country and practiced them. However, immigrant families usually tried to adopt the American lifestyle. They were determined to embrace new lifestyles and capitalize on opportunities that would help them build better families. They mainly focused on the future rather than the challenges they were facing.

The best way to understand Stan Lee's extended family and parents is to look at the larger group of Europeans and Jews who moved to NYC in the early years of the 20th century. Young Stan and his family members had similar experiences as other Jewish people and families that were trying to adapt to the new American life. All immigrants were trying to fit in.

In 1910, Jacob and his relative Abraham lived with a 52-year-old man from Russia named Gershen Moskowitz. That old man lived on Manhattan's Avenue A with his wife Meintz. His wife was actually a Romanian. They had two children, Rosie and Joseph. Both Joseph and Abraham were listed during the census, meaning they were probably working in the same shop. According to the census information collected at that time, both Liebers went to school and understood the English language, just like Moshkowitz's children. However, there were no additional details. The family and the people around them probably used Romanian Yiddish as their language of communication.

In 1920, Jacob was a 34-year-old man staying in a boarding home with David Schwartz, 26, and his 25-year-old wife, Beckie. The family lived with three young children on Manhattan's 114th Street. They had left Romania for America in 1914. Unlike Jacob, the Schwartzs were not conversant with the English language. However, there was a strong bond between immigrants because they worked together and even shared their private lives. David and Jacob managed to secure jobs in the growing dressmaking industry. Their house was located in a predominantly Jewish neighborhood with immigrants from Romania and Russia. This explains why Yiddish was the most spoken language compared to English at that time.

Jacob's life took a different turn two years later. The Schwartzs were his close friends and family in 1920, but he got married to a young woman named Celia Solomon in 1922. Before welcoming the New Year, Jacob and Celia had already been blessed with a newborn baby, Stanly Martin.

Generally, there is limited information about the Liebers and Celia Solomon's family tree. However, the few sources we found indicated that the Solomon family was relatively large and had immigrated to the U.S in 1901. In fact, the Solomons are a great example of what typical Jewish immigrants experienced as they tried to reach America in the 20th century. The entire family immigrated to America, which was a very expensive process for Jewish families who were having difficulty in saving money to run away from their own country. However, they didn't care because the only important thing was to keep the family intact even during hardships.

By 1910, the Solomons were living on 4th Street. The building they lived in was actually occupied by many families from Romania. Various documents use different first names for Celia's parents. Her father's first name was either Zanfer or Sanfir, while her mother's first name was either Sophie or Sophia. According to information from different sources, Sanfir and Sophia were born in 1865 and 1866, respectively. Robbie was the youngest and the first to born in the U.S.

There is no clear information about the exact year of Celia's birth, but it's believed that she was born in 1892 or two years later. In 1910, she started off as a seller in a dime store. Her brother Louis, who was older than her, also worked as a seller at a trimming store. They two never went to school, but her four younger siblings (Isidor, Minnie, Frieda, and Robbie) attended school while living with their family. Celia and her brother worked hard to feed the family and kept their siblings in school. The children portrayed the lives of young people from successful immigrant families.

Like other immigrant families from Romania and other European countries, the Solomons managed to settle in the U.S. Their aim was to live better and capitalize on the available educational opportunities. They were also willing to adopt popular culture despite having their own cultural norms and strong family values. Sanfir and his wife spoke Yiddish, but their children learned to speak the English language, which allowed them to adopt the new culture. After some time, the Solomons relocated to the West 152nd Street.

Around the same time, Stan Lee's family relocated to Washington Heights from West 98 and West End Avenue. His brother Larry was also born around the same time in October 1931. The decision to relocate presented a number of challenges with regard to the neighborhood and fortunes. Like other families during the Great Depression, the Liebers faced many challenges in an attempt to achieve the American Dream. It seemed like everything they were working for was gradually running away from them.

Chapter 2:

LIFE IN NEW YORK

On Manhattan's 29th Street outside the local Episcopal Church, about 2,000 men could be seen with their collars turned up. The wind was cold, so they had to keep their hands warm in their deep coat pockets. This was a common trend on the streets of Manhattan as the people of America welcomed the Great Depression. These men gathered around the church, hoping to get some of the food that was being distributed to the poor. They were extremely desperate and scared because there was hardly enough food for anyone. In fact, many people had to endure cold nights without eating anything to satiate their hunger.

It was quite demoralizing for city residents to see their fellow New Yorkers suffer because of poverty. The country was experiencing a serious decline in economic activity and those who queued in lines to receive bread and handouts did it against their will. They had to endure psychological torture just to feed themselves and their families. It was a difficult task, but they needed food, clothing, rent, medical supplies, and money.

The highly mismanaged Wall Street brought the country's economy down, leading to extremely depressed and annoyed residents who had to accept aid reluctantly. America was a wealthy nation in the 1920s when investment bankers and stockbrokers were booming. They were the new celebrities of that era. We are talking about people like the character portrayed by Nick Carraway in The Great Gatsby. Unfortunately, Wall Street was no longer stable, and the stocks went down. The economy also went down because of greed and trading exploits in the country.

Men became desperate, and that is why there were soup lines of men on the streets of Manhattan. This was a bad sign of the nation's economic crisis and countrywide despair. In fact, every person queuing for the food, and handouts represented a suffering family broken by the economic crisis.

Like other families, the Liebers had to endure the devastating effects of the Great Depression after building a better life in the U.S for several years. At that time, Stanley Lee was still a youngster and couldn't understand what was happening to his family. However, he was old enough to notice that his parents were suffering. He had vague memories of his father and mother trying to figure out where to get rent money from. Many families had to struggle every day for basic needs and worry about constant eviction notices. Luckily, the Liebers managed to stay without getting evicted.

The stocks went down in the last months of 1929. At this time, Jacob had already lived in the U.S for over 20 years. However, there was no form of protection for him and other workers during the financial crisis. The economic problem was so severe that he lost his job. Stan Lee remembered a time when his devastated father tried to run a diner and failed. Unfortunately, the diner took up all of his father's savings.

Jacob and Celia also faced significant challenges because of the lack of jobs. There was almost a new struggle every day, leading to a shaky marriage. Young Stanley saw his father and mother argue incessantly just because of money.

Interestingly, the radio was a great source of peace because the family would gather and listen to it without any fight.

Stanley was always happy to see his family members stay together in peace. The fights were more frequent during his early years. Romanian families always value close family bonds, which was also an important factor during the years of the Great Depression. Many parents allowed their children to attend school instead of allowing them to be laborers.

Stanley was fascinated by the works of Edgar Bergen, one of the most talented ventriloquists. Bergen used to perform on the Chase and Sanborn Hour on NBC with his wooden sidekick Charlie McCarthy. It was difficult for radio listeners to see that Bergen's sidekick was actually a dummy, so the most important thing about Bergen was his comedy skills and ability to create captivating characters.

Usually, Celia stayed at home, taking care of domestic tasks. On the other hand, Jacob looked at the ads and often went to the city, hoping to secure a job. He would return home every evening, looking exhausted physically and mentally. Sometimes he seemed extremely angry and hopeless than the other days. Stanley remembered how his father sat at the table, staring at nothing. He simply saw his depressed father watch the family go down because of the economic crisis. Sometimes Jacob tried to convince his wife to take the family to the park, but she would always refuse.

Like other families with limited financial resources, the Liebers was eventually forced to look for a smaller house in the Bronx. Stanley's bed was a coach in the family's living room. The living room of any low-rent house was usually situated in the back area. There was a window, and the only thing Stan could see was another building. The Lieber family lived in an overcrowded neighborhood, which was another challenge in addition to the lack of food to feed the entire family.

Chapter 3:

FAMOUS FIGURES

Cartoonists were among the celebrities of that time, but they were considered to be minor celebrities. One of the most famous people was cartoonist George Herriman, the creator of the American newspaper comic strip Krazy Kats. He had a brief encounter with art movements like surrealism and Dadaism.

The most popular and successful genres for fans of pulp magazines included romance, fantasy, and crime. The end of World War I marked the beginning of new title releases. These were generally cheap magazines featuring prototypes and fast-passed stories of comic superheroes such as the Spider, Buck Rogers, Tarzan of the Apes, and the Shadow. The pulps were a good source of inspiration for the creation of comic books with a flawless storytelling style. They also created a distribution path for comic books.

Reprinted collections were issued as early as 1897. However, their success was hindered by the fact that they were not original. They were also not colorful. However, the reprints presented a new market that was yet to be exploited. The opportunities were limitless, and the only challenge was the lack of affordable materials that could help writers in reaching the audience.

The market managed to take off in 1933 when Max Gaines and Harry Wildenberg of Eastern Color Printing Company in Waterbury discovered a new and marketable format. Their first publication was a 32-page magazine featuring colored reprints of Sunday strips. The magazine was sold to the

Procter & Gamble company. When it proved to be a success, Gaines decided to produce more magazines targeting corporate sponsors.

Gaines realized that people loved the comic strip collections, and perhaps they wouldn't mind paying for them either. In 1934, the Famous Funnies was used as the trial issue. It was a 10¢ periodical with a print run of 35,000 copies. Luckily, all the copies sold out. The sequel to the magazine was released in May that led to the inception of monthly series of comic books. This milestone marked the beginning of one of the largest industries in America.

Famous Funnies was basically a combination of previously printed newspaper strips like "Mutt & Jeff" and "Joe Palooka." However, the magazine didn't look like the modern-day comic book, the funny aspect of the book needed to be fine-tuned. Malcolm Wheeler-Nicholson, a former pulp magazine writer and a retired cavalry officer, happened to be the right person for that job.

New Fun Comics was the first feature with the format of a comic book. It was released in 1935, thanks to the efforts of Wheeler-Nicholson. The magazine focused on humorous, western tales and stories. Although it didn't bring a lot of sales, it played a crucial role in the history of comic books. Newspaper strip publishers usually charged high fees, but things were different for comic book companies.

The legend Harry Chesler opened the famous "Chesler Shop," which was a great success in the history of comic art. Young artists and writers got inspiration from the shop. The first people to work at Chesler Shop included Charles Biro and Creig Flessel. At that time, young Joe Shuster and Jerry Siegel were still waiting for the big break. Wheeler-Nicholson published their fictional superhero Dr. Occult, featuring a private investigator. Siegel joined hands with Shuster to produce more stories for comic books, but it was difficult to keep the fire burning.

Wheeler-Nicholson decided to collaborate with Jack Liebowitz and Harry Donenfeld to form the modern-day DC Comics. In 1937, Liebowitz and Donenfield bought out Nicholson when he faced a financial crisis. Today, DC Comics is one of the most successful American comic book publishers.

Chapter 4:

THE HERO IS BORN

Stan Lee grew up reading many stories featuring attention-grabbing characters. He would find the stories in comic strips, books, and magazines of his youth. Stan recollected how various heroic characters and their cruel enemies became an important part of his life. However, it took him some time before he could discover the origin of the "hero."

The Hero in Greek Mythology

During his school years, Stan Lee found Greek mythology heroes to be interesting for various reasons. First, ancient Greek stories focused on gods and demigods. Second, some of those stories included impressive poems such as "The Odyssey" by Homer. According to Stan, that blend of literature helped him realize that the hero was a word from ancient Greek. It simply referred to a demigod who was mortal and a god's offspring. Humans built worship cults around heroes who were mainly mentioned in oral history before they appeared in written stories and poems.

A Sumerian named Bilgames was the first epic hero to be recognized in the oldest writings even before the ancient Greek heroes. He was later renamed to Gilgamesh, who became the 5th king of Uruk (Iraq) in 2500 BC. Bilgames appeared as the main character in the earliest surviving epic poem from Mesopotamia, the Epic of Gilgamesh. In the poem, Bilgames is a demigod and the son of a goddess (*Ninsun*) and a mortal (*Lugalbanda*).

The term hero continued to appear in texts for hundreds of years. It was mainly used to denote fearless characters with powers that enabled them to overpower their enemies. Even today, the hero is a courageous character who is ready for the challenge and is determined to do what is considered to be right. If you read heroic stories, you'll realize that the hero does what is good for everyone in society. In the early years of heroic tales, the hero was mostly a character with excellent fighting skills, but things kept changing over the years. The hero of today can do all sorts of things virtually, in any setting.

Heracles (or Hercules as we know him) is one of the greatest ancient Greek mythology demigods. His name simply means the glory or pride of Hera (queen of Olympian gods). The irony is that many stories about him show how the queen tortured him.

The famous Greek poet Homer got inspiration from existing heroic stories to create his epic poem, the Odyssey. In the poem, the gods' interference did not stop Odysseus from bringing his fighters home after the war. He actually shot several axes with an arrow! It was an incredible skill in addition to other resourceful qualities that helped him create the famous Trojan horse.

In general, there are many stories explaining the origin of heroes. Some of these stories are stranger and more complicated than the others. It was a common trend to hear about a future hero through prophesy. There were also stories of people trying to kill unborn heroes. In the latter case, parents would try to hide and brought up their children in secret. A good example is the story of Moses. Pharaoh's wife found the abandoned child and decided to raise him.

When Moses grew up, he was the hero who saved enslaved Jews from the hands of the cruel Egyptian ruler.

Greek mythology texts describe Hercules as Alcmene and Zeus' son. Alcmene was considered to be the wisest and most attractive mortal woman. However, Zeus was Hera's husband, so Hera was angry with her unfaithful husband. During one of her angry moments, Zeus put the infant Hercules near her breasts, and she breastfed him. As a result, Hercules became partially immortal and gained a lot of strength.

The Evolving Hero

The hero has evolved over the years. Let's take a look at history to see how ancient writers helped the hero evolve. The world's first highly civilized cultures included the cultures of ancient Babylonia and Mesopotamia. Humans were compared to stars whose lives were based on a perpetual mathematical formula. The king symbolized the sun while the cosmos represented the Mother Goddess, who gave life to humans.

However, things changed after the arrival of the Semites and Indo-European Aryans. Each of these cultures brought its own mythology dominated by male figures. Their fighter gods symbolized thunder.

Those tribes managed to survive because of the incredible technology and skills of ironsmiths. Their mythologies eventually blended with their subjects' mythologies leading to a weaker Earth Goddess. Since then, Greek, Indian, and Persian culture mythologies started to thrive. A good example is when the

Greek god Zeus became the god of thunder when the Greeks were defeated by the Romans. After their victory, the Romans were able to steal some aspects of Greek mythology and culture.

Thanks to the new form of male-dominated mythology, characters who seemed weak were downgraded. For instance, the wine god Dionysus was reduced to a demigod. The new type of mythology was also responsible for ancient biblical stories that featured less powerful female characters. For example, Eve deserved to be worshiped in ancient cultures, but she was easily lured by a snake.

More nations were dominated by males, including Japan. For instance, the Japanese god Hachiman was based on the divine Emperor Ôjin. It's said that the so-called god of war died and was born again amongst men as a god. Similarly, Zeus was the father of men and gods in the earliest Greek religion at Olympia. He was also the thunder god in Greek mythology.

Female Heroes

Interestingly, the first hero to be recorded was actually a woman. She was the priestess of Aphrodite and the love goddess. She developed feelings for a man named Leander while in Hellespont where she lived. However, she couldn't marry the love of her life because of chastity vows. Leander had to swim to Europe from Asia with the help of Hero's tower lamp. Unfortunately, the young man drowned when an unprecedented storm extinguished the lamp.

The Hero was unable to withstand the pain, so she decided to throw herself into seawaters and lost her life. This changed some of the aspects of a hero making, and people realized that a hero doesn't necessarily need to be glorious.

The Greek term *"he‾ro‾s"* didn't turn into the English term we know today until the year 1387.

Heroes in Different Parts of the World

Heroes have been around for many centuries, and there are various heroic figures in different parts of the world. Gods were often regarded as heroes in ancient nations like Greece, Japan, China, Egypt, and Ireland. Writings that could be traced back to the 9th century have described rich Celtic myths. They were simply oral stories presented in written form. Those included Lebor, Gabála, Érenn, and stories of Balor of the Evil Eye and Tuath Dé Danann. The latter defeated Balor after several battles and took over the land. Such Irish legends were retold several times, turning the Tuatha into a magician population.

Other heroes were created through the years to meet people's desire to be saved from tyranny and fear. Many of them appeared in the stories taking on mythological proportions. For instance, the British leader King Arthur is remembered for leading the rebellion against the Saxon invaders. Arthur managed to stay on the throne and is remembered for his heroic quest. It's said that his own people betrayed him, and he ended up losing his life in a battle.

The French received and accepted the stories, but they realized that they needed to create their own character. They decided to create the incredible Lancelot, who had an adulterous relationship with Arthur's wife, Queen Guinevere. The story of Arthur was retold several times and prompted archeologists to look for evidence of this historical figure. As Arthur's story spread throughout France and England, the Germans were also consolidating stories featuring Norse supernatural beings. By 1100 AD, Sigurd or Siegfried had gained popularity. Richard Wagener used the legendary hero in his operas 7 centuries later.

Ordinary People Becoming Heroes

Over the years, the character of the hero changed. Ordinary people who can do amazing things are now considered to be heroes, regardless of their gender. Anyone can now become a hero based on the decisions of those in power or their achievements on the battlefield. In the book *"On Heroes, Hero-Worship and the Heroic in History,"* written by Thomas Carlyle in 1841 was mentioned mere mortals such as Frederick the Great and Oliver Cromwell. On the same note, Alexander the Great was also considered a hero.

The Hero's Fall and Death

One of the most fascinating things about heroic stories is that heroes usually have dramatic deaths or falls. A good example is Robin Hood's death, which happened in a battle. The most interesting part is that he actually located his own burial place by shooting an arrow. If you look at most stories involving heroes, you'll notice that no one can replace them. Heroes are just unique in their own way.

Chapter 5:

THE ORIGIN OF COMICS

Comics have been around for many years, thanks to the cumulative work of the writers who worked hard over the years. Just like the writing process, comics have undergone a process that has taken several years to bring out the best. Humans have been telling stories using pictures since the era of cavemen. The earliest humans to live in caves painted images of their conquests and successful hunts.

Hundreds of years passed, but humans still used pictures as a method of communication. They learned how to develop languages using pictures as demonstrated by the beautiful hieroglyphics found in ancient Egyptian temples as well as pyramids. In ancient countries such as Korea, Japan, and China, people created pictures and represented objects using simple brushstrokes. The simplified pictograms were quite attractive. Humans were able to use well-crafted images to tell stories about their religion. In Europe, people learned how to create scrolls with images to improve the reader's experience. Those pictures made the scrolls more interesting to read.

During the early years of the 18th century, humans were already creating magazines and newspapers with illustrations to make their fiction more interesting. The Adventures of Mr. Obadiah Oldbuck is considered to be the oldest publication in the history of American comics.

Comic Strips

Over time, the comics industry experienced a significant change because of the development in advanced printing technology. That technology allowed publishing companies to print newspapers with colored images. Richard Outcault (Yellow Kid) is one of the earliest cartoon characters to be printed using colors. In fact, Richard Outcault was the first popular character to reappear in comic strips. The new printing technology led to an unexpected level of success, which led to merchandising, particularly after the character's debut in 1895.

Comic strips were able to make the most of everything that was already available to create something new and to entertain the audience. Newspaper publishers tried everything possible to reap from popular features. Over time, comic strip creators managed to make profits and became popular.

Stanly Lee was born in 1922 when comic strips were already popular and could be found in almost every paper. At that time, comic strips spread across several pages and were larger than the modern-day comic strips. Large images made the pages look stunning and allowed the artists to produce detailed artwork that captured the reader's attention with ease.

According to Stan Lee, he used to read the comic strips, but he wasn't as passionate as his friends were. His favorite comic strips included Krazy Kats by George Herriman, Red Barry, They'll Do It Every Time, and Skippy. In addition to reading comic strips, Stan would read anything he could. He believed that writers needed to read in order to familiarize themselves with various genres and learn how to tell stories in different ways.

Stan Lee started reading books when he was still a young boy. His passion for books led to his discovery of the legendary Shakespeare and his love for the author's writing skills and language. However, he was more excited to read magazine stories featuring pulp hero stories with instinctive quests. The bright colored magazine covers also made him love the stories. Stan would watch a number of films whenever his family finances allowed him. The family would also come together and listen to some interesting comedy and adventure radio programs.

Many newspaper publishers took advantage of comic strips to attract the attention of many readers. They made more money by including collections of several popular comic strips. Book collections for comic strip lovers also emerged by the year 1901. Before Stan Lee was born, people were already selling these collections in different parts of the country, like in train stations and several cities.

The American publishing company Cupples & Leon is one of the companies that used to package and sell those collections. They played a crucial role in developing the modern-day comic books. The next big breakthrough happened in 1929 with the introduction of The Funnies by George Delacorte. The Funnies was a 24-page tabloid with mixed colors. Copies of the publication were sold on newsstands for a dime. Although the publication faced challenges for 36 issues before collapsing, Delacorte became famous for establishing Dell Publishing.

Chapter 6:

THE HISTORY OF COMIC BOOKS

According to most historians, Famous Funnies is considered to be the first comic book in the modern comic book industry. Since the inception of the book, Harry Wildenberg teamed up with other creators in 1934 to create more comic strips. Wildenberg worked for the Eastern Color Printing Company in Waterbury as a salesman.

That company was the leading printer of the best Sunday sections with colorful images, so it was easy to find new formats. Wildenberg played a vital role in turning comics into retailer premiums, starting with the popular Gulf Oil Company. Such premiums contributed to the creation of folded newsprint sheets with 64 tabloid-sized pages. The package came with a cover and was stapled before selling.

While at the Eastern Color Printing Company, Wildenberg worked with Max Charles Gaines, who was one of the pioneering figures in the creation of the modern comic book. The two were able to sell many premium comics on newsstands. They decided to do things differently by selling their premiums to children for a dime. Gaines also worked with Delacorte to create the Funnies.

The year 1935 was the year of breakthrough for comic books because Famous Funnies made huge sales. This brought stiff competition in the industry, and

Gaines decided to package Dell's popular comics after seeing the industry's potential.

Major Malcolm Wheeler-Nicholson is another famous figure in the history of comic books. He was initially a soldier before he decided to become a pulp writer. The comics industry presented a great business opportunity to him, so he decided to create original material for comic book readers. He wanted to create something he could own without spending money on the license fees required by newspaper organizations. His New Comics turned out to be the company's first release that became the famous DC Entertainment.

The industry continued to grow at an incredible pace providing children with new and more entertaining content. Many people also saw the industry's business potential and were eager to capitalize on the opportunities like Martin Goodman, who was Stan Lee's relative. At the age of 16, Stan Lee was helping Goodman to write comics. Goodman's publishing company produced pulp magazine covering all the topics, including science stories and western topics. He was always alert and ready to make the most of the latest trends. This allowed him to steer new trends and stay ahead of the competition.

Detective Comics introduced a new feature during springtime in 1938. Goodman believed that the feature would revolutionize the industry. At that time, Detective Comics was already a successful company after releasing three titles. The company was making plans for the next big feature, Action Comics. Gaines of Eastern Color sent one of the rejected materials from Joe Shuster and Jerry Siegel, who were writing science fiction and detective stories. The young cartoonist who would later become an editor - Vincent Sullivan loved the new character, so he decided to create a cover featuring Superman.

As years went by, there was an increasing demand for costumed heroes with bright colored attire, chests that could withstand bullets and evil characters around them. Goodman realized that it was the right time to focus on the comic book industry. Of course, he needed people to take the industry to the next level, so he looked for artists and writers to fill 64-page titles. He bought the necessary materials from studios before becoming self-sufficient. After some time, Goodman decided to bring the Sub-Mariner character back to life. That character appeared in Bill Everett's promotional Funnies Weekly and was different from the Man of Steel. Goodman was doing well with the character.

In 1939, the feature appeared in Marvel Comics #1 for the first time together with the original Human Torch by Carl Burgos. Joe Simon came from another studio to become an editor. He came with the young and talented Jack Kirby, with whom he collaborated to create Captain America.

Soon after, the 17-year-old Stan walked in, hoping to work for his relative for some time before venturing into real writing. What happened next was beyond his expectations. He ran errands before becoming a temporary editor and eventually became a publisher.

Almost all children were already devoted fans of comic books. Even farm boys who turned into soldiers would read comic books on their way to combat. Artists and writers had to work hard to meet the increasing demand for comic books even in the final years of the economic crisis. Superheroes influenced readers to purchase war stamps and look for scrap metal.

There was an increasing number of fascinating genres in the late 1940s. These included romance, crime, horror, funny animals, and teen sensation. Those who visited newsstands could find Archie, Millie, and other famous characters alongside Captain America, Batman, and Captain Marvel. Writers and artists probably tried to write a comic book based on every imaginable idea. Stan Lee considered the trend to be a great learning opportunity. Sometimes Martin asked Stan and his colleagues to stop working on certain books to write another. Switching from one project to another was the order of the day, and so the writers, editors, and artists had to adapt.

Challenges Faced by Stan and Other Comic Writers

It wasn't a smooth journey for the creators of comic stories because of the challenges that arose later. Parents were worried about the effects of comics on their children. In fact, some parents accused comics of turning their children into juvenile delinquents. For this and other reasons, Congress had to hold hearings focusing on comic books, radio, TV, and films.

There was also a significant decrease in sales forcing the remaining publishers to work together under William Maxwell Gaines's son. There was an attempt by Bill to stand against the union. However, he ended up being outvoted, leading to the development of the Comics Code Authority and the Comic Magazine Association of America. That was the beginning of the distribution of safe comics with no violence or horror.

Stan had to let some people go because of the changes that took place. It was a difficult decision to make and one of the hardest moments of his life. Shortly after, Martin decided to switch distributors, which was not a good decision after all. The team got stuck following the fall of American News and Martin partnered with Independent News, DC Comics' sister company. However, the team was only able to produce 8 books in a month, forcing Martin to have 16 monthly titles covering all genres.

Meanwhile, the editorial team at DC Comics was trying to bring back their declining Flash in a Showcase issue. Sales started to go up, so he appeared 3 more times before returning to his title. DC managed to revive several characters and was eventually able to create captivating superheroes and succeed in the business. The market was already full of many characters who came together to create the Justice League of America.

Martin was aware of Justice League's sales, so he decided to order a new title for a superhero. With encouragement from his wife Joan, Stan was able to create the team he was excited to read. He worked with the gifted Jack Kirby to produce the Fantastic Four. Luckily, they were able to attract the attention of readers and even contribute to the formation of the Marvel Universe.

In the 1960s, Marvel introduced several compelling heroes and was still competing with the growing DC Comics. There was a significant increase in the number of publishers as well as children (Baby Boomers) who bought comic books. At the time, children who read comic books were educated individuals looking for more leisure and diversions. The works of Stan Lee and his colleagues were a great source of diversion.

Chapter 7:

STAN LEE'S FAMOUS WORKS

Throughout his career as a comic book writer, publisher, editor, and producer, Stan Lee managed to create many captivating comic superheroes. Before he passed away in 2018, he had been the primary creative leader for Marvel Comics for two decades. He created some of the industry's most interesting comic superheroes and partnered with famous comics like Jack Kirby and Steve Ditko to create various successful superhero characters as we know them today. His memories live in our minds, and every cameo in Marvel movies will always remind us of him.

Famous Characters Created or Co-Created by Stan

Stan Lee is famous for taking part in the conceptualization and creation of hundreds of characters. In this section of the chapter, we will focus on some of the most successful characters he helped create.

Spider-Man

Fans of comics and experts in the comic industry will tell you that Spider-Man, the alias of Peter Parker, is one of the most successful characters to be created by Stan Lee in collaboration with Steve Ditko. This fictional superhero first appeared in the comic book *Amazing Fantasy #15* in 1962. Since then, Spider-Man has found his way in various films and successful comic books published by Marvel Comics.

His creators gave him a wide range of superpowers and skills including the ability to cling on walls, maintain balance in awkward positions, sense danger, and moving faster than a normal human being. Spider-Man also boasts intellectual skills that allow him to make decisions and act like a genius. Another fascinating fact about Spider-Man is that he has worn different types of costumes, which include the red and blue suit, the symbiote suit, and the black cloth suit. His suits usually have a spiderweb design. Spider-Man stories have won several awards since 1962.

The first and the longest Marvel comic book series featuring Spider-Man is *The Amazing Spider-Man* series. It features other characters that Stan helped create, namely Jonah Jameson, Mysterio, Scorpion, Sandman, Norman Osborn, Vulture, Doctor Octopus, Rhino, Shocker, and Prowler.

X-Men

In 1963, Stan Lee partnered with artist Jack Kirby to create the X-Men, a team of superheroes who appeared in comic books published by Marvel Comics. The X-Men first appeared in *X-Men #1* in September 1963. The original members of the team included Beast, Cyclops, Iceman, Jean Grey, and Angel. *X-Men #1* also featured Professor X and the team's archenemy Magneto. Since then, the X-Men have appeared in various books, movies, TV shows, and even video games. Most X-Men stories revolve around time travel, space travel, fate, death, resurrection, and fictional locations.

The X-Men are human mutants with superpowers that allow them to fight for equality and peace. The mutant gene gives them a wide variety of powers. These powers include flight (from wings, sonic scream, telekinesis, magnokinesis, and weather manipulation), teleporting, wall-crawling, body transformation, self-duplication, elasticity, explosive energy charges, fire and heat manipulation, superhuman speed, strength, reflexes, senses, and mental abilities.

Fantastic Four

The Fantastic Four is Marvel's first family featuring Sue Storm, Johnny Storm, Reed Richards, and Ben Grimm. This team was created by Stan Lee in conjunction with Jack Kirby, and its characters first appeared in *Fantastic Four #1* in 1961. It's a cohesive team of characters who stand with each other in times of crisis. Although there have been several lineup changes, the most frequent lineup features Mister Fantastic (a science genius), Invisible Woman (Mister Fantastic's girlfriend/wife), the Human Torch, and The Thing.

The fictional superhero team has appeared in comic books published by Marvel Comics and has been the subject of several animated TV series. The team has also inspired the creation of film characters such as the amazing characters in *Fantastic Four* (2005 and 2015) and *Fantastic Four: Rise of the Silver Surfer* (2007). Members of the team have also appeared in video games like Questprobe (1985), Fantastic Four video game (1997), Spider-Man video game, Marvel: Ultimate Alliance, Marvel: Ultimate Alliance 2, and Pinball FX 2 by Zen Studios.

The team has faced various enemies over the years, and these include the Mole Man, the Skrulls, Doctor Doom, Klaw, Annihilus, Puppet Master, Blastaar, Psycho-Man, Dragon Man, Diablo, Terminus, Red Ghost, Impossible Man, Super-Apes, and Terrax the Tamer.

Hulk

Hulk is one of the oldest characters created by Stan Lee and Jack Kirby. The fictional character first appeared in the first issue of "The Incredible Hulk" in May 1962. In comic stories, the Hulk is a green-skinned, muscular humanoid with a lot of physical strength, which is usually proportional to his anger level. His durability and endurance are also proportional to his temper. The hulking green man has the power to resist damage and possesses regenerative, adaptive, and healing capabilities.

Iron Man

Iron Man is another fictional superhero appearing in Marvel's Comic books. The character was co-created by several individuals, namely Stan Lee, Larry Lieber, Jack Kirby, and Don Heck. He first appeared on the cover of *Tales of Suspension #39* in 1963. However, he got his own title in May 1968. Initially, Stan Lee used Iron Man to explore Cold War themes, but later adaptations focused on contemporary issues. Iron Man is one of the original members of the Avengers, and he has appeared in several comic books, TV shows, and films including *Iron Man* (2008), *Iron Man 2* (2010), *Iron Man 3* (2013), *The Incredible Hulk* (2008), *The Avengers* (2012), *Avengers: Age of Ultron* (2015), *Avengers: Infinity War* (2018), *Avengers: Endgame* (2019), *Spider-Man: Homecoming* (2017) and *Captain America: Civil War* (2016).

Like many fictional superhero characters, Iron Man has a powered armor that grants him weapons and superhuman powers such as flight, strength, and durability. His superhuman abilities also include enhanced healing powers, brain-controlled armors, and enhanced technopathy. You should watch one of the aforementioned movies to witness these and more powers.

Black Panther

Black Panther (T'Challa) is another incredible fictional superhero brought to us by Stan Lee and Jack Kirby. He first appeared in *Fantastic Four #52* in 1966. Black Panther is portrayed as the protector of the nation of Wakanda. He has made numerous appearances in television shows, animated movies, and video games. Chadwick Boseman has portrayed Black Panther in *Captain America: Civil War* (2016), *Avengers: Infinity War* (2018), *Avengers: Endgame* (2019), and *Black Panther* (2018). In fact, the 2018 *Black Panther* movie is one of the highest-grossing movies of all time.

Other characters that Stan Lee helped create include Daredevil, Ant-Man, Thor, Doctor Strange, Inhumans, Blob, Toad, Sentinel, Scarlet Witch, Galactus, Silver Surfer, Supreme Intelligence, Owl, Gladiator, Vanessa Fisk, Happy Hogan, Mandarin, Madame Masque, Whiplash, Fenris Wolf, Volstagg, Mangog, Destroyer, Absorbing Man, Clea, Brother Voodoo, Kaecilius, Mephisto, Triton, Lockjaw, Maximus, Karnak, Giant-Man, Goliath, Bill Foster, Wasp, Egghead, Groot, Sharon Carter, Man-Thing, Living Tribunal, Falcon, and Wonder Man.

Stan Lee's Cameos

In addition to being a great comic writer and editor, Stan Lee also appeared in some of the best movies featuring the characters he helped create. This section focuses on some of the best Stan Lee cameos, which include the last one - *Avengers: Endgame*.

The Trial of the Incredible Hulk (1989)

Stan Lee's first cameo was as a jury member in *The Trial of the Incredible Hulk*. In that movie, Banner was wrongly accused of sexual assault. Daredevil (Matt Murdock) was in his case, and Stan Lee could be seen in a courtroom during the trial. The enraged Hulk tears things apart during the hearing, forcing the jury members to run away for their lives. The scene was Stan's first appearance in a live-action TV or film project associated with Marvel Comics.

X-Men Movies

Besides creating the founding members of the X-Men, Stan Lee also appeared in the 2000 movie with the same title as the group. That was one of the shortest Stan Lee cameos, but it was fascinating to see the famous comic writer act alongside other actors in the scene. The scene was shot at the beach with Stan acting as a hot dog vendor. Senator Kelly emerges from the sea as a mutant, and everyone on the beach is surprised to see him, including Stan Lee.

In *X-Men: The Last Stand* (2006), Stan appeared in one of the most exciting scenes in the movie. In that short scene, the older man could be seen busy watering his garden using a hose only to be surprised by the superpowers of Jean Grey. When Magneto and Professor X visited Jean Grey, her superhuman capabilities affected her neighbors. She had the power to lift objects from the ground, like cars and Stan Lee's hose.

In *X-Men: Apocalypse* (2016), the powerful mutant Apocalypse was bringing down destruction affecting the lives of millions of people. People around the world, including Stan and his wife, were looking up in fear.

Spider-Man Movies

Spider-Man is one of the most loved characters to be created by Stan Lee. Stan simply couldn't afford to appear in other films and failed to appear in a Spider-Man film. In the 2002 *Spider-Man* film, he had a cameo during the battle between Spider-Man and the notorious Green Goblin. As debris fell from the buildings, Stan was one of the people caught up in the crowd. He appeared briefly to save a young girl from falling objects.

It seems Stan's cameo in *Spider-Man 2* (2004) was inspired by the scene in the 2002 movie. It's all about saving innocent people from falling debris during Spider-Man's battles. In the 2004 movie, Stan appeared during the fight between Spider-Man and Doctor Octopus to save a woman from the falling debris. However, Stan appeared in a completely different situation in *Spider-Man 3* (2007). He came across Peter Parker, who was walking through Times Square. Stan stood next to Parker and said, "You know, I guess one person can make a difference." The two were looking at a sign with the words "Spider-man to receive the key to the City."

Stan also appeared in *The Amazing Spider-Man* (2012). It was a funny scene where Stan was wearing headphones and was completely unaware of the battle between Spider-Man and the Lizard. Two years later, Stan had another cameo in *The Amazing Spider-Man 2* (2014). Stan appeared as one of the people who had attended Peter and Gwen Stacy's graduation.

Stan loved his Spider-Man character so much that he had to appear in *Spider-Man: Homecoming* (2017). In that scene, Spider-Man was busy with his crime-fighting activities when he accidentally attacked an innocent man whom he thought was trying to steal a car. The car's alarm alerted the neighbors as well as Stan Lee. The old man looked outside through the window giving Spider-Man a warning for the disturbance.

Iron Man Movies

Just like the famous Spider-Man movies, Stan made several appearances in several Iron Man movies. He had a cameo in *Iron Man* (2008), where he appeared in a red-carpet scene surrounded by gorgeous women. People thought he was Hugh Hefner. His cameo in *Iron Man 2* (2010) occurred during the Stark Expose. It was funny because he was mistaken for Larry King. He actually looked like Larry with his signature suspenders. Stan had another cameo in *Iron Man 3* (2013), where he appeared as a beauty pageant judge. He could be seen on a TV set, giving one of the contestants 10 points.

Guardians of the Galaxy (2014)

In *Guardians of the Galaxy*, Stan could be seen talking to a young woman while Rocket spies on him through his scanning device. Rocket described Stan as a pervert.

Captain America Movies

Stan appeared briefly in *Captain America: The First Avenger* (2011) in a gathering of people who were waiting to see and honor Captain America. He mistook another man for Captain and said he expected the Captain to be taller. In *Captain America: Civil War* (2016), Stan appeared at the end of the movie. The scene was at Tony Stark's door, where Stan appeared as a deliveryman from FedEx holding a box. In *Captain America: The Winter Soldier* (2014), Stan worked as a security guard at the Smithsonian Institute. Captain America stole Stan's suit, and Stan was seen saying, "Oh man, I am so fired."

Black Panther (2018)

Stan Lee appeared in *Black Panther* as a high-roller gambler. Before he appeared on the screen, T'Challa, Okoye, and Nakia were in a casino trying to capture Ulysses Klaue. When T'Challa left to deal with the bad guys, Stan took the opportunity to steal his winnings.

Avengers Movies

Being one of the creators of Avengers, Stan Lee, appeared in various Avengers movies. In *The Avengers* (2012), the city of New York was devastated, and Stan appeared during a news report. In *Avengers: Age of Ultron* (2015), Stan acted as a war veteran who could be seen enjoying some drinks with the Avengers. There is a Stan Lee cameo in *Avengers: Infinity War* (2018) as well, where he could be seen driving a school bus carrying Peter Parker. Stan also had a posthumous cameo in the 2019 *Avengers: Endgame* movie. He appeared as a 1970's car driver, and that was his last cameo in any Marvel movie.

Stan also made appearances in other films including *Daredevil* (2003), *Hulk* (2003), *Fantastic Four* (2005), *Fantastic Four: Rise of the Silver Surfer* (2007), *The Incredible Hulk* (2008), *Thor* (2011), *Thor: The Dark World* (2013), *Big Hero 6* (2014), *Ant-Man* (2015), *Deadpool* (2016), *Doctor Strange* (2016), *Guardians of the Galaxy Vol. 2* (2017), *Thor: Ragnarok* (2017), *Ant-Man and the Wasp* (2018), *Venom* (2018), *Ralph Breaks the Internet: Wreck-It Ralph 2* (2018) and *Captain Marvel* (2019).

Final Years and Demise

Like any other person, Stan had his own challenges before he passed away. In September 2012, he underwent surgery to insert a pacemaker. His wife Joan passed away in 2017 at the age of 95 due to complications caused by a stroke. On 12th November 2018, Stan was rushed to Cedars-Sinai Medical Center in Los Angeles, where he died later that day after a cardiac arrest. May his soul rest in peace.

Conclusion

Stan Lee is undoubtedly one of the most successful comic writers and editors in America and the world at large. Reed Richards was his first unconventional superhero character with unique traits. Instead of creating the usual good-looking character with strong muscles, Stan created a thin character with the brains of an intelligent scientist.

Stan understood the need for a female superhero and created Sue Storm as one of the members of the famous Fantastic Four team. However, the two characters didn't make the kind of team he wanted, and so he added two more characters. Those were Sue's younger brother Johnny Storm and a strongman named Ben Grimm. The new characters created more tension in Stan's stories that helped him grab the attention of more readers. At last, readers were able to choose their favorite superhero character from the team.

During the early years of his career as a professional comic writer and editor, Stan got inspiration from the Cold War, atomic and nuclear tension. People were afraid of a nuclear attack, making it a great topic to write about. While cruising to space, cosmic rays gave Fantastic Four the powers that allowed them to perform unusual feats. They combined their forces to fight together for society's wellbeing.

Stan was a great writer, but he also faced many challenges in addition to his devastating childhood experiences. He would often scrape and cancel his stories. He wanted to write stories that could attract young and adult readers. For that reason, his stories were based on teammates who worked together as family members. He finally managed to create characters and write stories that every reader could relate to regardless of their age.

The Fantastic Four played a crucial role in saving Stan's career by paving the way for other amazing characters and stories discussed in that book. The team also saved Americans and marked the beginning of comic books in America and the world at large. Evidently, the comic world will always appreciate his works and remember him as a talented comic writer, editor, producer, actor, and publisher.

Printed in Great Britain
by Amazon